Introducing
CATS

Introducing
CATS

by

ALAN C. JENKINS

F.R.G.S., F.Z.S.

SPRING BOOKS

LONDON

Published by

SPRING BOOKS

SPRING HOUSE · SPRING PLACE · LONDON NW5

Broadly speaking there are three possible attitudes to cats: indifference, hatred and love. We need not spend much time over the first. Clearly there must be something lacking in anyone who can fail to be moved in some way by the animal whose name is one of the first words we learned to spell in those far-off days when the magic of language was being revealed to us. A, T—AT; C—AT—CAT; C—A—T spells CAT.

It might be questioned in passing whether 'cat' itself is a particularly adequate word for a creature that has so many smooth, sinuous characteristics, the sleek softness of its fur that crackles waxily with electricity when you stroke it in front of the fire, the rounded contentment of its purr, the sinister suppleness of its movements as it pretends it is in the jungle.

Its wild cousins have been given far more resounding names which echo something of their character. The lion, for example—one can hear a faint menacing roar in the dipping chasm of the syllables. Tiger, equally, if you linger on the first syllable, brings a breath of startled fear, the deer poising in panic-stricken hesitation. Panther, snow-leopard, jaguar... even lynx with its hint of narrowed eyes glaring down from some forest bough, all these words conjure up their picture.

In comparison how ordinary, how terse is the word cat. Yet after all perhaps that is as it should be; perhaps the word does express something neat and efficient and it is certainly a much pleasanter word than 'dog', with its connotation of something rather dejected and skulking at heel.

*   *   *

But we were talking about attitudes, not words.

As for hatred, for many people it is as difficult to understand anyone hating or shall we say detesting cats, as it is to think of his being indifferent to them. Yet there are cases even of men clambering on to chairs or tables when a cat enters the room, just as women are supposed to take refuge at the sight of a mouse.

Evidently there is something repellent either about the noiseless insinuating movements of the cat or the superb glossiness of feline fur that these people cannot bear; as of course others cannot endure the touch of feathers. One can only suppose that these unfortunates who react so violently to cats must in a former life have been mice or rats or some other rodent species which had sound reason for fearing or hating the cat who

> ... rejoices with quick leaps
> When in his sharp claws sticks a mouse!

There is in addition another category of hatred; that of the gardener who, livid with fury at the sight of a ravaged seedbed, lays abominable traps consisting of potted meat jars with a smear of bloater paste on the rim and foul ammonia at the bottom to be snuffed up by the next unfortunate cat. (Yet in the countryside the cat is more often the tireless ally of the gardener, guarding his peas against the forays of mice and voles, his lettuces against the attacks of Peter Rabbit's surviving relations.) The bird-lover, too, is moved to savage imprecations or tears, as the case may be, when some treasured visitor, bullfinch or goldfinch or robin, is murdered, insult being added to injury by its being deposited as a gift on the hearthrug.

The sufferer from insomnia raises his head from the pillow in despair as the local 'moggies' start their marvellous eldritch hymn of hate. Even the housewife who tends the cat has her moments of doubt when her loose covers or Indian rug are used for the purpose of sharpening claws, preparatory to a walk down the garden path.

*   *   *

As for loving cats, the word love is probably the most abused in the entire English language which, like the English countryside, has suffered unkind treatment at the hands of those who use it. By implication 'love' should be—well, one of the loveliest of words, but it has been debased, it has lost its purity and is now used to embrace anything from an admiration of, say, Dirk Bogarde to a taste for liquorice allsorts.

At the risk of arousing the ire of fanatical 'cat-lovers' (a term which, I must confess, makes me wince), it must be said that it has also been misused in regard to cats. The word love in this instance should be divided into a number of shades, including fondness, liking, respect, admiration, even obsession: for it is perfectly possible to become obsessed by cats, and there are many examples of this, from the sad case of Louis Wain who could do nothing but draw cat-faces until he drew one too many and went mad as a result, to old ladies—or François Coppée, the poet, for that matter—who allow their swarming pets the run of the dining-room table.

The most elementary form of love for the cat is summarized by the nursery rhyme with which children once grew up (do they now, I wonder, or are they taught couplets about baby spaceships and lonely sputniks?):

> I love little pussy,
>   Her coat is so warm,
> And if I don't hurt her,
>   She'll do me no harm.
> So I'll not pull her tail,
>   Nor drive her away,
> But pussy and I
>   Very gently will play.

This of course is an admirable and very English approach and is undoubtedly the reason why many people love cats, because they are soft and lissom and cuddly, a symbol of what some people would like life itself to be, instead of being jagged and harsh; though others like the cat because of its very contrariness, its silky warmth contrasted with its marvellous retractable claws—which in fact are much more reflective of life.

*   *   *

But the true cat-lover, as we must say for want of a better word, likes the cat for other reasons than the silkiness of its coat, the apparent bonelessness of its ways. The true cat-lover's attitude is tempered by admiration and respect. Respect, indeed, is one of the most ancient of reactions to the cat. The ancient Egyptians venerated cats, painted them in company with their Pharaohs. They wondered at the cat's astonishing eyes and fancied that these waxed and waned in accordance with the phases of the Moon. They even deified cats and embalmed them with reverent care when they died.

In the Middle Ages cats were considered so valuable that a cat-tariff was established by law. Even before it opened its eyes a kitten was valued at one penny. Tuppence was the price of an older kitten, while a cat that had already caught its first mouse was worth as much as fourpence, a considerable sum in those days. Heavy penalties were imposed on anyone who killed a cat from the Royal granaries.

Perhaps all this is the key to what our attitude to cats should be: we both respect and value the cat. We value it for the very practical work it does for us. It is estimated that there are at least as many rats as there are human beings: one shudders at the thought of how many there would be if cats disappeared entirely. As for mice...

We value the cat for the company it gives us, for the homeliness of its friendly tapping at the window, for the perfect little machine of its purr, and above all for that picture of security and warmth and cosiness summed up in the fact that:

> Puss loves man's winter fire
> Now that the sun so soon
> Leaves the hours cold it warmed
> In burning June.

We respect it for that mysterious, independent life it leads: man has never entirely conquered his fear of the dark and there is something little short of magic in creatures that can so easily find their way about by whisker and eye in that other world of the night. Besides, the cat's own attitude is so eminently sensible: unless we are stupid we don't always want to be clinging round the necks of human beings we love. We soon cloy their love if we do not allow them out of our sight.

Thus, unlike the dog who has acquired some of our nastiest characteristics, the cat possesses many of the best human qualities (or should that smug statement rather be inverted?): it comes and goes without fuss. It is not above using a little flattery, which all of us like; it makes fond little gestures when it wants attention, like H. G. Wells's cat that used to touch him on the cheek with a paw. It is ready in good time for friendship and, one might well say, conversation and even a little song. But, like a model guest or friend, it does not outstay its welcome. The visit, the ritual, over it takes itself off on its secret ways and certainly Kipling's Cat-who-walked-by-himself was typical of his kind. He accepted a bowl of milk as fee for the work he did, but he never gave up his independence.

How unlike the dog and the horse is the cat in this respect. The dog's pathetic servility is, like the poor before the days of the Welfare State, always with us; while as for the horse, the trouble is you have either to jump on its back or put it in the shafts or have a bet on it.

But the cat perhaps has never forgotten that she was once a goddess and behaves accordingly, being at once beautiful, benign, enigmatic, aloof, letting no man know too much about her.

The cat's origins are as mysterious as its ways. The dog and the horse, we know, roamed wild tens of thousands of years ago. The caveman painted the wild horse on the walls of his home and hunted it for its flesh before he learned to tame and ride it. The dog skulked jackal-like round human settlements and adopted man.

But the cat has never been associated with primitive tribes. It is essentially a creature of civilization and nobody seems to know whence it really came. As far as Britain is concerned it was brought by the Romans (who had got it from the Egyptians), along with the ass and the pheasant and the fallow-deer.

The main reason for the cat's independent character is of course its natural antecedents. The dog, descended from the race of jackals and wolves, was used to going in packs and having a leader. Man has become its leader and that is why it looks up to him so; whereas the cat, probably descended from the wild-cat of Africa, was always solitary by nature and went its own individual way.

Not only was the cat venerated in Egypt, it was also a friend of the family, sitting with them at mealtimes and accompanying them on hunting expeditions as many ancient paintings show.

It was a capital offence to kill a cat in Egypt and there is a record of a Roman soldier being put to death for such a crime. Legend has it that when the Persians invaded Egypt they once approached a fortress bearing cats in their arms, anticipating that the Egyptian soldiers would not attack them for fear of hurting the cats, one of whose forbears was the cat-goddess Bast, goddess of life, maternity and happiness.

Whatever the association of the Moon with its eyes, it is easy to see that the cat came from a land of the Sun. Nothing is more redolent of drowsy languor than a cat basking in the sunshine.

It is perhaps strange that despite the cat's distinguished history in ancient Egypt, no Egyptian breed has been developed, unless the Abyssinian cat can claim that lineage. The aristocracy of cats moved to Siam and here, too, cats dwelt freely in the temples. This came about because the souls of the noble dead were believed to take up residence in cats, so that upon the death of a member of the Royal family one of the palace cats would be taken to the temple to act as a kind of reception committee for its new occupant. Nowadays there are more Siamese cats in London than in Siam.

Siamese cats are not always as peaceful as this picture suggests. The toms are notable fighters and fight with a terrible fury, particularly against 'lesser breeds without the law'.

The origin of the Siamese cat's incomparable blue eyes is, according to legend, due to the fact that once when cats had defended a temple altar against the sacrilege of a barbarian enemy, the priests prayed that as a reward heaven should thereafter be visible in the cats' eyes... and as we know this prayer was granted!

Cats have so many facets to their character, so many expressions. From the pot-pussy cat face that is the epitome of self-satisfaction, to the meditative which, sphinx-like, seems to conceal so many mysterious, age-old thoughts and memories. From the anxiously anticipative to the frankly replete; from the ingenuous to the wistful. From the sociable to the aloof; from the indifferent to the alert.

8

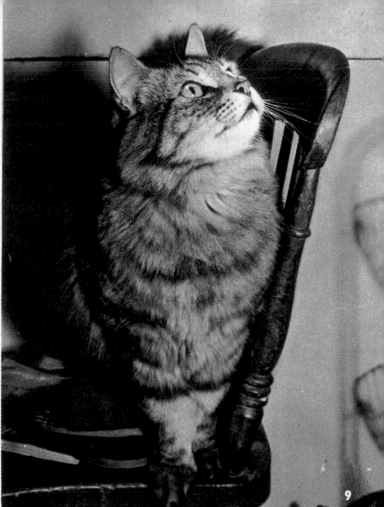

9

10

11

'Cats', wrote Edward Topsell in his seventeenth century *Historie of Foure-footed Beastes*, 'are of divers colours, but for the most part grizelled, like to congealed ice, which cometh from the condition of her meate: her head is like unto the head of a Lyon, except in her sharp ears: her flesh is soft and smooth: her eyes glitter above measure especially when a man cometh to see a cat on a sudden, and in the night, they can hardly be endured, for their flaming aspect. Wherefor Democritus describing the Persian smaragde saith that it is not transparent but filleth the eye with pleasant brightnesses, such as in the eyes of Panthers and Cats, for they cast forth beames in the shadow and darkness, but in the sunshine they have no such clearness and therefore Alexander Aphrodise giveth this reason, both for the sight of Cattes and Battes, that they have by nature a most sharp spirit of seeing.'

It is the infinite variety in the character of the cat that endears it to us. It is elegant but eminently useful; it loves the warm hearth equally with the excitements of the chase. It is composed yet sensitive; it retains its independence yet is genuinely affectionate. It can be savage when need be, yet delicate and exquisite. Its talons can rend like a razor, yet its coat has the quality of silk. It has a sense of fun, as when it chases its own tail or the autumn leaves, yet a sense of decorum, too.

Its ways are fastidious, its movements the essence of effortless precision. There is the moment when it becomes 'one breathing trembling purr', as Harold Monro put it, and another when its voice is like that of a soul in torment. Its attitude towards us ranges from a soft lovingness that is more than merely animal, to that bland inscrutability we can never penetrate. It is this mixture of cosiness and mystery that is irresistible.

The word cat is believed to originate from the Latin *cattare*, to see, a pleasing association of ideas. The Egyptians, on the other hand, used a beautiful onomatopoeic word for the cat, namely, 'Mau'.

17

18

Are all cats grey in the dark?
  Emphatically not.

Obviously a cat like this, descendant of the temple guardians, should be in the top drawer.

Some Siamese cats have a kink in their tail, a characteristic due, according to legend, to the fact that one day when a Siamese princess went bathing she gave her ring to her cat to guard. The handiest place to put it was on its tail and the kink was the result of the cat's anxiety to make certain the ring did not fall off.

21

The dog bears its master's name on its collar; the horse submits to the bridle and the spur. But the cat comes and goes at will.

And sometimes a cat just wants to be left alone.

Unhappily no fewer than a quarter of a million cats have to be destroyed every year by the R.S.P.C.A. There are estimated to be six million cats in Britain and there is a natural increase of nearly 750,000 a year.

Too many cats, perhaps, for the cat breeds readily and prolifically: witness the case of the Exeter tabby which had more than 1,200 identified progeny in little more than ten years.

24

25

If nobody can truly 'own' a cat, a cat will often adopt a human being. One of the most famous examples of cat friendship was in the case of Sir Thomas Wyatt. Imprisoned in the Tower of London during the Wars of the Roses, Wyatt was befriended by a cat which used to bring him pigeons it had caught. According to Horace Walpole he 'was preserved from being starved' by this act of mercy!

Edward Topsell knew all about feline wiles. 'It is needless to spend any time about the Cat's loving nature to man, how she flattereth by rubbing her skinne against one's legges, how she whurleth with her voyce, having as many tunes as turnes; for she hath one voice to beg and to complain, another to testifie her delight and pleasure, another among her own kind by flattring, by hissing, by spitting, insomuch as some have thought that they have a peculiar intelligible language among themselves.'

26

Leigh Hunt, too, essayist and critic and friend of Shelley, Keats and Byron, observed the cat well:

'Poor Pussy!' he wrote in his essay *The Cat by the Fire*, 'she looks up at us again, as if she thanked us for those vindications of dinner; and symbolically gives a twist of a yawn and a lick of her whiskers. Now she proceeds to clean herself all over, having a just sense of the demands of her elegant person—beginning judiciously with her paws, and fetching amazing tongues at her hindhips. Anon, she scratches her neck with a foot of rapid delight, leaning her head towards it, and shutting her eyes, half to accommodate the action of the skin, and half to enjoy the luxury. She then rewards her paws with a few more touches; look at the action of her head and neck, how pleasing it is, the ears pointed forward, and the neck gently arching to and fro. Finally she gives a sneeze, and another twist of mouth and whiskers, and then, curling her tail towards her front claws, settles herself on her hindquarters, in an attitude of bland meditation.'

28

'What cat's averse to fish?' the observant poet remarked.

Alas! fish, like curiosity, have sometimes got the cat into trouble. The most famous case was Thomas Gray's 'favourite cat, drowned in a tub of gold fishes'.

'Twas on a lofty vase's side,
　Where China's gayest art had dyed
The azure flowers that blow;
　Demurest of the tabby kind,
The pensive Selima reclined,
　Gazed on the lake below...

Unfortunately, poor Selima

　...tumbled headlong in;
Eight times emerging from the flood
　She mewed to ev'ry wat'ry god...

But in vain!

This cat, however, was luckier. Having put his head inside a goldfish bowl he was rescued from a similar fate in the nick of time. Here he is wearing the glass rim of the jar round his neck. What happened to the goldfish when the jar was smashed is not recorded.

Other cats are sensible enough to get somebody else to do their fishing for them!

Selima was not by any means the only cat celebrated in poetry. Keats addressed a sonnet to a cat:

> Cat! who has passed thy grand climacteric,
>   How many mice and rats hast in thy days
> Destroy'd?—How many tit bits stolen? Gaze
>   With those bright languid segments green, and prick
> Those velvet ears—but pr'ythee do not stick
>   Thy latent talons in me—and upraise
> The gentle mew—and tell me all thy frays
>   Of fish and mice, and rats and tender chick.
> Nay, look not down, nor lick thy dainty wrists—
>   For all the wheezy asthma—and for all
> Thy tail's tip is nick'd off—and though the fists
>   Of many a maid have given thee many a maul,
> Still is that fur as soft as when the lists
>   In youth thou enter'dst on glass bottled wall.

Imposing language, without doubt; but one cannot help feeling that Keats was more inspired by nightingales than cats.

Parson Woodforde, the eighteenth century Norfolk clergyman, once performed an operation on his cat:

'I had a poor little cat,' he recorded in his diary, 'that had one of her ribs broke and that laid across her belly, and we could not tell what it was, and she was in great pain. I therefore with a small pen knife this morning opened one side of her and took it out, and performed the operation very well, and afterwards sewed it up and put Friars Balsam to it, and she was much better after, the incision was half an inch. It grieved me much to see the poor creature in such pain before, and therefore made me undertake the above, which I hope will preserve the life of the poor creature.'

Fishing... or admiring his own reflection?

33

'All that night long Simpkin hunted and searched through the kitchen, peeping into cupboards and under the wainscot, and into the tea-pot where he had hidden that twist; but still he found never a mouse!'

The cat in this picture was luckier than the Tailor of Gloucester's, for if you look carefully you will see that he has got what he wants—'his supper of a little fat mouse'.

Is the cat cruel when he plays with his prey? Cruel perhaps in our eyes; but it is just as wrong to judge the cat or any other animal by our own standards as it is to assume it is dumb because it does not speak our language.

Rabbits have always held an irresistible attraction for country cats, but there were great dangers in this. The gin trap is now illegal in Britain, but there are still many three-legged veterans among cats to prove the hazards of the chase. My own black cat, who sits purring on my desk as I write this, was ten days in a trap, but now he hobbles round on a stump as nimbly as Long John Silver—though without a crutch.

38

The jungle, like time, is relative. In miniature there is as much fear and drama in the English hedgerow where the cat stalks the vole or the woodmouse as in the forests of India where the tiger lunges out at the sambur. Here an English tiger lies at ease after making his kill—and incidentally, what better example of protective colouring than this?

Pussy cat, pussy cat, where have you been?
I've been to London to look at the queen.

One Devonshire cat I knew travelled all the way to London and back in a day. It stowed away in a furniture van and refused to eat or leave the van until the return journey of more than four hundred miles was over. Perhaps it wanted to make certain its 'owners' were not moving house.

Or maybe it had heard that in some parts of the country it used to be considered unlucky to take the cat with you when you moved. This belief was probably fostered by someone who didn't want the trouble of getting the cat used to a new home. The traditional way of making certain that a cat doesn't stray from a new home is of course to butter its paws frequently. Presumably it will be so preoccupied in licking them that it will forget all about its worries. But obviously you have to keep it out of the drawing room while the treatment is being carried out.

This kitten clearly doesn't want to be left behind.

Some cats equally clearly like travelling.

Apart from constantly being accused of consorting with witches, cats have often had a tough time in the past, in spite of having once been goddesses. In Java during times of drought children would ceremonially duck a he-cat and a she-cat in the nearest river and then carry them in procession to the accompaniment of music.

This was mild compared with the treatment meted out to cats in France. Part of the traditional midsummer jollifications consisted of burning alive a sackful of cats in the bonfires round which people danced. This custom, the result of the cat being regarded as representing the devil (perhaps because of its earlier association with pagan gods), so horrified Louis XIII when he was Dauphin that he begged his father, Henry IV, to forbid it.

He did not seem to have succeeded in abolishing the custom, for his son, Louis XIV, not only approved of it but used to light the bonfire with his own hands.

At harvest time, too, a cat's life was liable to be in dire peril. For example, in parts of France a cat used to be killed to celebrate the cutting of the corn, while at threshing time a cat was put into the last sheaf and beaten to death by the flails. Afterwards it was roasted and formed the *pièce de résistance* of the celebratory supper.

That sort of talk is enough to make any cat look anxious.

44

'Our Dumb Friends' is surely one of the stupidest expressions, typical of the mantle of smug complacency human animals always assume. Because they do not speak our language it is certainly wrong to imagine that animals have no means of communication. What could be more conversational than this group of cats demurely discussing local events on their doorsteps?

As for these two, it is plainly a case of 'Have you heard this one?'—though whether it is enough to make a cat laugh is not recorded.

Some of us like the mantel-piece.

This is *my* chair.

The cat shouldn't need to lead a sheltered life, for it is reputed to have nine lives…

…but it has far fewer names. Most cats are of course given personal names, from Simpkin who belonged to the Tailor of Gloucester, to Columbine, Thomas Carlyle's pride. The poet Southey gave his cats positively exotic names such as Hurly-burly-buss and Macbum and Rumpelstiltskin.

There are numerous terms of endearment such as pussykins and tiddles, but strangely few folk-names. Little pigs, for example, are called by a variety of nicknames, from Little Josey to treseltrype and from greck to nisgal; yet the cat remains simply the cat—or puss, a name she shares with the hare. Only in Suffolk do they have special terms for cats. There a tom-cat is known as a jim-cat and a she-cat is a Betty-cat.

As Elizabeth Mary Wright suggested in her *Rustic Speech and Folklore*, perhaps the latter came about through an association of ideas, for the kettle in East Anglia used to be known as Betty… and the fire-loving cat would often keep it company by the hob.

However, though its nomenclature may be limited, the cat has had a great deal of attention paid to it in English sayings and proverbs which are an everyday part of our conversation, just as the cat itself is an everyday part of our lives.

We know, for instance, how true it is that a cat may look at a king, a sturdy Englishism indeed. Care killed the cat—in other words you die if you worry and you die if you don't; so why worry?

How expressive is nervous as a cat and what an excellent simile is a cat on hot bricks! Waiting to see which way the cat jumps is a favourite saying applied to politicians, though it should not be inferred from this that they are all rats or even mice. To grin like a Cheshire cat, to fight like Kilkenny cats... there is no end to the sayings. The cat has indeed taken an immortal place in our language.

In nursery rhymes, too, the cat has had a good press.

There is the rollicking story of:

> Hey diddle diddle,
>   The Cat and the Fiddle,
> The Cow jumped over the Moon,
>   The little Dog laughed
>   To see such sport,
> And the Dish ran away with the Spoon.

Then there is the near-tragedy of:

> Ding dong bell,
>   Pussy's in the well;

but fortunately Little Tommy Stout was at hand to foil the machinations of that nasty little Johnny Green.

> What a naughty boy was that,
> To try to drown poor pussy cat,
> Who never did any harm,
> And killed the mice in his father's barn.

There was also that famous trio who got into trouble:

> Three little kittens they lost their mittens,
> And they began to cry,
> Oh, mother dear, we sadly fear
> That we have lost our mittens.
>
> What! lost your mittens, you naughty kittens!
> Then you shall have no pie.
> Mee-ow, mee-ow, mee-ow.
> No, you shall have no pie.

Obviously this trio has been trying to find their mittens in the drawer.

It's all a matter of taste…

53

strong stuff…

milk…

54

…or just plain tap water.

We know that too much curiosity is bad for one, but the spirit of exploration is well developed in cats... though you're always liable to encounter formidable dangers in life.

57

58

59

Cats have impeccable manners. They don't bolt their food like some creatures we could mention—and they politely wait their turn, even when a dog has ungallantly barged his way in first

60

Cats share with the badger the reputation of being the cleanest of animals. Their personal habits are fastidious to a degree, unlike the uncouth dog whose greatest delight is to make himself thoroughly unpleasant by rolling in the nearest available carrion.

'As clean as a cat' is the most accurate of sayings and it is a fascinating sight to see that rough tongue rasping away at the cat's toilet.

62

..while some cats even go so far as to use the family bathroom for their ablutions, judging by these photographs.

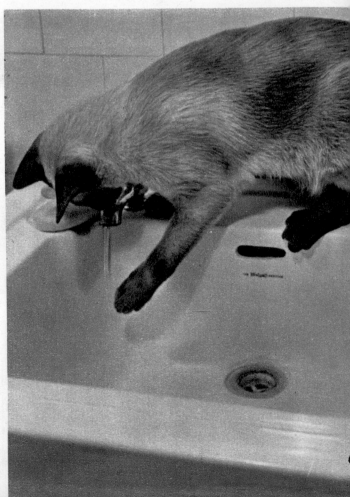

63

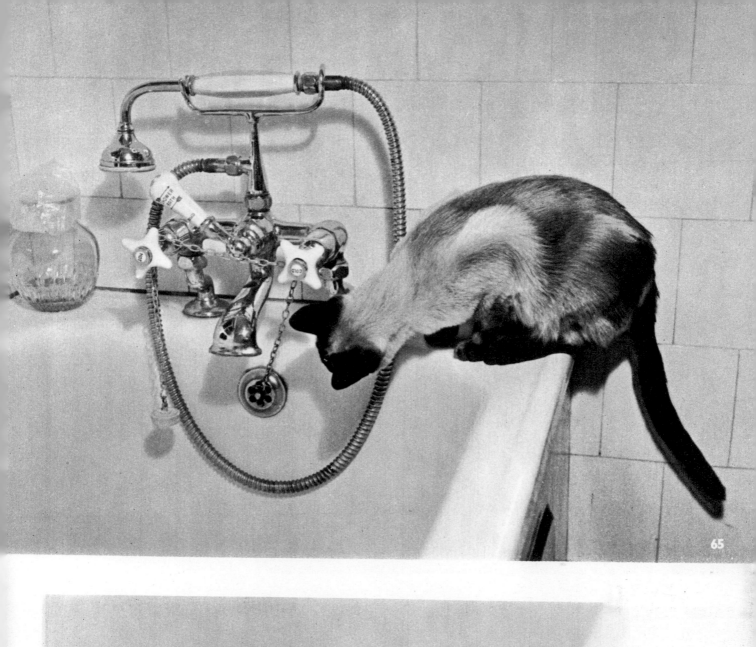

65

66

Because of its association with 'the heaped-up hissing blaze', we usually think of the cat sitting, hunched up, a neat bundle of fur, contemplating life, or curled in furry comfort in an armchair. Yet what a beautiful body it has when it goes into action to spring perhaps at a butterfly or a bird...

As it happens, this Blue Point was leaping at a shrimp dangled tantalizingly above it.

67

68

Two's company—quite affectionately so...

...three is clearly a crowd—very strained company indeed.

As an ex-goddess representing among other qualities the joy of maternity, the cat makes the most loving of mothers. Nothing is more delightful than the little chirruping purr with which she greets her kittens as she returns to her bed. She is a fierce mother, too, when need be, and will defend her young ones with fang and claw. She is fussy, too, and if her bed does not suit her she will remove the kittens one by one to a better place, picking them up gently in her teeth by the nape of the neck... exactly as her giant cousin the lioness will do.

If she has lost her kittens she will readily adopt other young creatures, and I have known a cat suckle baby otters and rear them successfully.

74

Though the kitten is born blind it needs no guidance in finding its way to its mother's life-giving milk.

75

..or to the milk-bowl later on!

This small white kitten was found as a stray in the local coal yard, and now waits to be collected by a kind new owner.

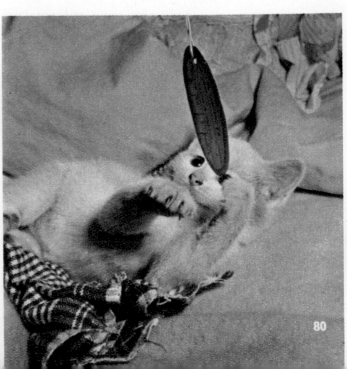

Cats at home...

...and abroad.

The term sea-dog has an honoured place in English history. It conjures up visions of Drake singeing the King of Spain's beard, of Grenville going to an heroic doom in the *Revenge*. Yet dogs actually rarely go to sea; on the other hand cats are often to be encountered in ships, but one never hears the expression sea-cat!

In his *Voyages*, Richard Hakluyt quotes an instance of a ship's cat going overboard: 'It chanced by fortune that the shippes Cat leapt into the sea, which being downe, kept her selfe very valiantly above water, notwithstanding the great waves, still swimming, the which the master knowing, he caused the skiffe with half a dozen men to goe towards her and fetch her again, when she was almost halfe a mile from the shippe, and all this while the shippe lay on staies. I hardly believe they would have made such haste and meanes if one of the company had been in like perill. They made the more haste because it was the patrons cat...'

B7

Undoubtedly that ship's cat used up one of its nine lives in the process. What is the origin of these supposed nine lives that cats proverbially enjoy? Is it perhaps through their intimate association with the first great Nine Gods of ancient Egypt who gave them their protection?

There is some disagreement on whether black cats are lucky or unlucky. Some people will make a detour to avoid having their path crossed by a black cat. I had a friend who one morning on his way to work saw a black cat scuttling across the road ahead of him, obviously with malice aforethought. In order to frustrate it, my friend broke into a run and to his satisfaction he managed to head the cat off. However, in doing so he found to his dismay that he had passed under a ladder without crossing his fingers. He therefore felt obliged to retrace his footsteps. As he passed under the ladder for the second time a pot of paint fell on his bare head and he was in hospital for four weeks with a fractured skull.

There is clearly a moral in this experience.

Certainly the black cat has got a dubious reputation to live down. Too close a connection with witches ('thrice the brinded cat hath mew'd') has occasionally made it suspect in the past. In some parts of England it is still believed that a black kitten born in May will bring bad luck; in Devonshire it was supposed to encourage vipers and other noxious creatures into the house.

Personally I can believe nothing but good of black cats and the nicest saying about them is that

> Wherever the cat
> of the house is black,
> Its lasses of lovers
> will have no lack.

89

90

91

Authors and poets have always been well known for their love of cats, which is very understandable, for the cat has an eminently soothing influence. It is, too, a contemplative creature and sits silent and companionable, thinking its own enigmatic thoughts as the author grapples with his own.

> A poet's cat, sedate and grave
> As poet well could wish to have,

wrote William Cowper, who was devoted to both kinds of puss, the cat and the hare.

Edward Lear had a cat named Foss which lived seventeen years. Andrew Lang delighted in the mystery of cats and was convinced they dreaded death with almost human perception. Sir Philip Sidney had 'a great white nimble cat, a king upon a mouse'. Pierre Loti considered that cats *'ont des petites âmes ombrageuses, des petites âmes de calinerie, de fierté et de caprice...'* ('are easily offended — they have little souls which may be in turn caressing, haughty and capricious...'). W. H. Hudson wrote of the cat as the largest-brained and most perfect mammal.

One of the most famous literary cats was Dr Johnson's Hodge. Boswell complained that he 'frequently suffered a good deal from the presence of the same Hodge. I recollect him one day scrambling up Dr Johnson's breast, apparently with much satisfaction, while my friend, smiling and half-whistling, rubbed down his back, and pulled him by the tail; and when I observed he was a fine cat, saying, "Why, yes, Sir, but I have had cats whom I liked better than this"; and then, as if perceiving Hodge to be out of countenance, adding, "but he is a very fine cat, a very fine cat indeed".'

Not only authors, but great men of all degrees have appreciated the company of cats. One of the most famous 'great men' cats was the friend of Sir Richard Whittington whom the bells bade 'turn again, turn again'. Philologists, however, now tell us that the mayoral fortune was not due to a cat but to *acat* or *achat*, in other words merchandise, probably coal.

But the legend—and the pantomime—will persist, whatever the authorities say.

Sir Isaac Newton, ironically unscientific for once, had two holes cut in the door of his room, one large, one small, so that his cat and kitten could come and go at will. Cardinal Wolsey is said to have had his black cat sitting next to him on the woolsack when he administered justice, though that may have been a nasty rumour put about to show he was in league with the powers of evil.

93

Kitten...

...and more kittens.

98

Cats have often had their portraits painted. Cardinal Richelieu never had his own done without his favourite cat Racan being included. Hogarth painted

a most striking cat in his portrait of the Graham children. Sir Winston Churchill's marmalade cat was drawn by Sir William Nicholson.

Izaak Walton, in *The Compleat Angler*, quotes Montaigne, the sixteenth-century French essayist:

'...as the learned and ingenious Montaigne says like himself freely, "When my cat and I entertain each other with mutual apish tricks, as playing with a garter, who knows but that I make my cat more sport than she maketh me? Shall I conclude her to be simple, that has her time to begin or refuse to play as freely as I myself have? Nay, who knows but that it is a defect of my not understanding her language (for doubtless cats talk and reason one with another) that we agree no better? And who knows but that she pities me for being no wiser than to play with her, and laughs and censures my folly for making sport for her, when we two play together?"'

Edward Topsell again:

'This beast is wonderful nimble, setting upon her prey like the Lyon, by leaping: and therefor she hunteth both Rats, all kinds of Myce, and Birds, eating not only them, but also Fish, wherewithal she is best pleased...'

And a catnip mouse is useful for keeping your hand—or claws—in!

102

The cat is indeed the symbol of the home. Mark Twain summed this up when he wrote in *Pudd'nhead Wilson* that 'a house without a cat, and a well-fed, well-petted, and properly revered cat, may be a perfect house, perhaps, but how can it prove its title?'

104

When the tea is brought at five o'clock,
And all the neat curtains are drawn with care,
The little black cat with bright green eyes
Is suddenly purring there.

(Harold Monro: *Milk for the Cat*)

These cats haven't waited for tea-time—but perhaps black cats are more patient?

105

One of the most sensible and admirable traits the cat possesses is its knack of always finding a comfortable place.

106

107

We are exhorted to 'let sleeping dogs lie'. The prophet Mahomet believed in applying the adage to cats as well. He was apparently so fond of his cat (said to have been called Muezza) that once when it was drowsing in his arm and he had to go out, he cut off the sleeve of his gown rather than rouse the cat from its slumbers...

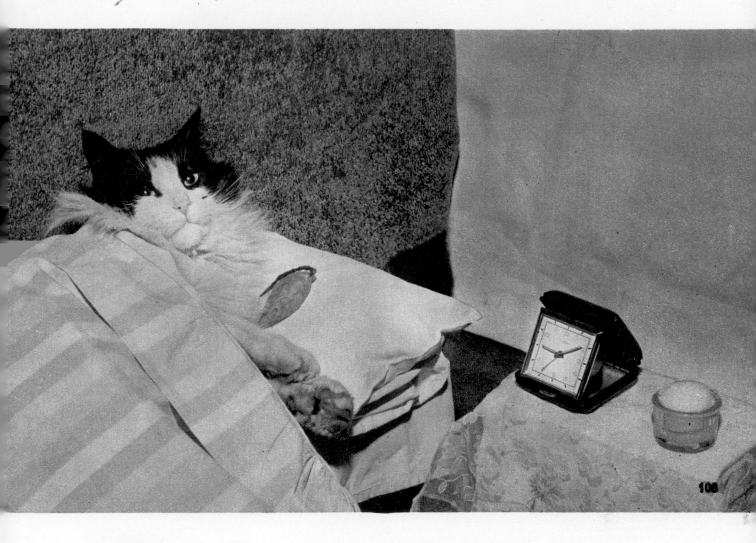

...this cat, however, likes to be called on time.

109

Indifference is another of the typical characteristics of the cat. If only we could occasionally turn our backs on the news as this cat does. Unfortunately the world is too much with us, whereas the cat sensibly believes in enjoying life while it can.

110

For a cat there are some things even more important than books—washing is one of them.

Too many cats in the world? Surely not, if they were all as beautiful as us!

ACKNOWLEDGEMENTS

Acknowledgements are gratefully made to Mrs Harold Monro for permission to quote the first verse of *Milk for the Cat* from the COLLECTED POEMS of the late Harold Monro; to the Literary Trustees of Walter de la Mare and Faber & Faber Limited for permission to quote the first verse of *Puss;* and to the following for permission to reproduce original photographs: Miss Jane Burton, plates 3, 4, 27, 61, 76, 77, 78, 79, 80, 81, 91, 93, 94, 96, 97, 100, 101; Heron Carr Esq., plates 28, 52, 58, 104; C. H. Cook Esq., plates 1, 2, 8, 42, 83; Patrick Coulsan Esq., plate 107; D. G. Davis Esq., plate 56; Mrs D. W. Durst, plates 84, 85, 95; Ian H. C. Fraser Esq., plate 88; The Rev. C. W. Gibbons, plates 14, 15, 57, 75; Mrs M. E. Giles, plates 7, 12, 13, 21; Anthony V. Gregory Esq., plates 9, 10, 11, 47, 59, 60, 103; Mrs S. Hare, plates 71, 98, 99; E. T. B. Hicks Esq., plates 5, 20, 45, 46, 67, 68, 69, 92; Mrs. M. E. Hulett, plate 105; Miss Elsie Jeffries, plates 17, 25, 40, 102, 106; Kemsley Picture Service, plate 30; Miss Mary Love, plates 16, 38, 86, 110; Miss Sheila Lowndes, plates 55, 62, 63, 64, 65, 66 (photographs by D. A. Wright); Mrs A. St. J. Maggs, plate 19; Anthony Robinson Esq., plates 73, 74, 82, 87 (photographs by Dr Josephine Bittner); The Royal Society for the Prevention of Cruelty to Animals, plates 23, 29, 32; B. E. Van Steenwijk Esq., plates 72, 90; Mrs D. Wemys, plates 6, 31, 48, 50, 53, 108, 111; Lieut.-Col. O. G. W. White, D. S. O., plates 18, 34, 35, 36, 37, 51, 109; Miss M. Wight, plates 33, 39, 41, 44, 54, 70; Mrs Celia Williams, plates 22, 24, 26, 43, 49, 89 (photographs by H. Collins).

Printed in Czechoslovakia

T 566